It's never too late to play...
CHRISTMAS

17 NEW ARRANGEMENTS FOR PIANO SOLO AND DUET

PAM WEDGWOOD

© 2006 by Faber Music Ltd
This edition first published in 2006 by Faber Music Ltd
Bloomsbury House
74–77 Great Russell Street
London WC1B 3DA
Music processed by Jeanne Roberts
Cover designed by Shireen Nathoo
Printed in England by Caligraving Ltd
All rights reserved

ISBN10: 0-571-52652-7
EAN13: 978-0-571-52652-9

To buy Faber Music publications or to find out about the full range of titles available
please contact your local music retailer or Faber Music sales enquiries:

Faber Music Limited, Burnt Mill, Elizabeth Way, Harlow, CM20 2HX England
Tel: +44 (0)1279 82 89 82   Fax: +44 (0)1279 82 89 83
sales@fabermusic.com   fabermusic.com

Contents

Let it snow! Let it snow! Let it snow!	4
We wish you a merry Christmas	5
Past three o'clock	6
In dulci jubilo	7
White Christmas	8
Il est né le divin Enfant	10
Coventry carol	12
Ding, dong, merrily on high	14
Walking in the air	16
In the bleak midwinter	18
Santa Claus is comin' to town	20
Quem pastores laudavere	22
Christmas song	24
The Virgin Mary had a baby boy	26
Adeste, fideles	28
Silent night	29
Winter wonderland: duet	30

Let it snow! Let it snow! Let it snow!

Words by Sammy Cahn
Music by Jule Styne

© 1942 Cahn Music Company Warner/Chappell North America, London W6 8BS
Reproduced by permission of Faber Music Ltd. All Rights Reserved

We wish you a merry Christmas

Traditional English carol

Past three o'clock

Traditional English carol

In dulci jubilo

Traditional German carol

White Christmas

Words and music by Irving Berlin

© 1954 Irving Berlin Music Corporation Warner/Chappell Music Ltd, London W6 8BS
Reproduced by permission of Faber Music Ltd. All Rights Reserved

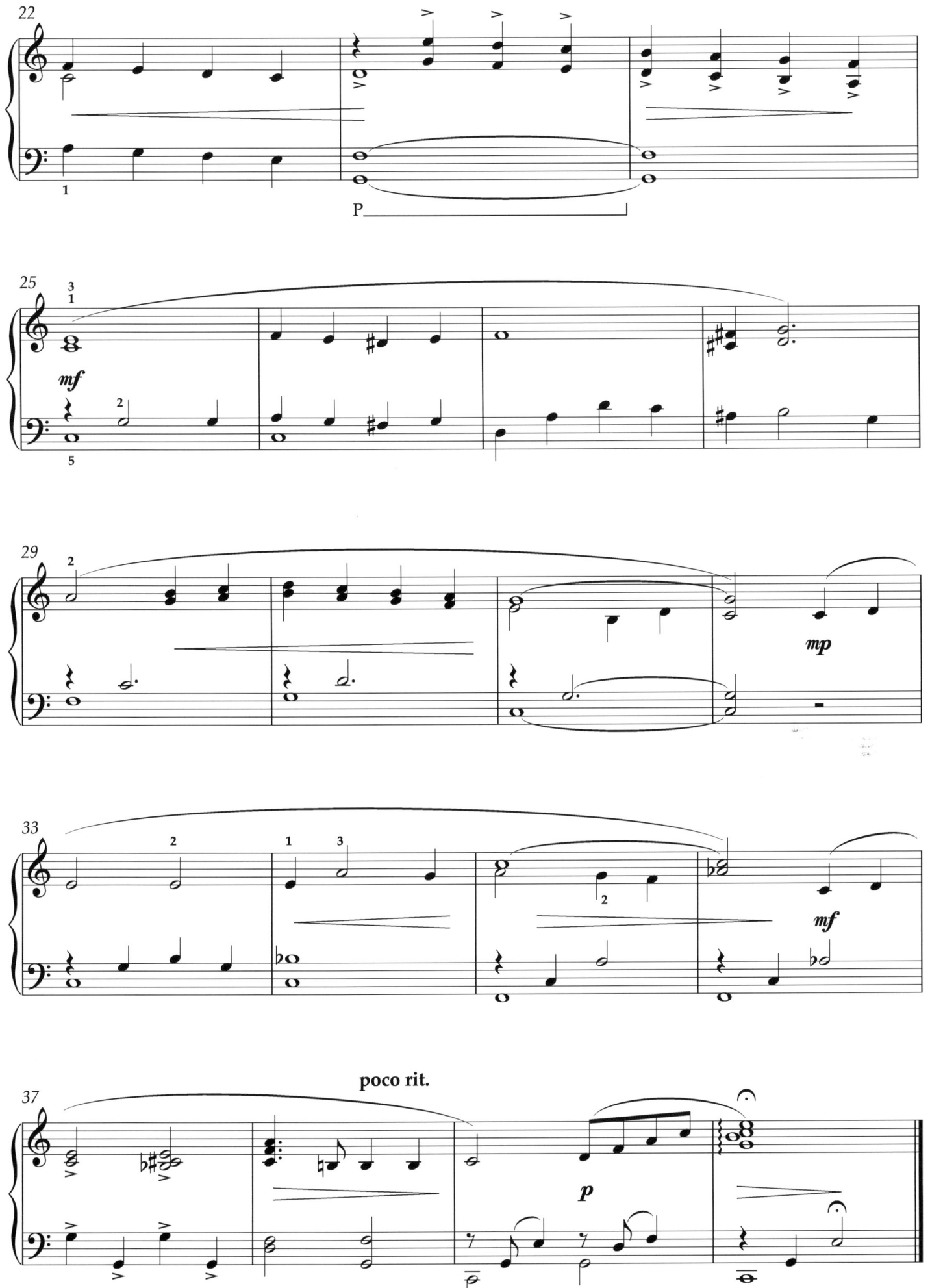

Il est né le divin Enfant

Traditional French carol

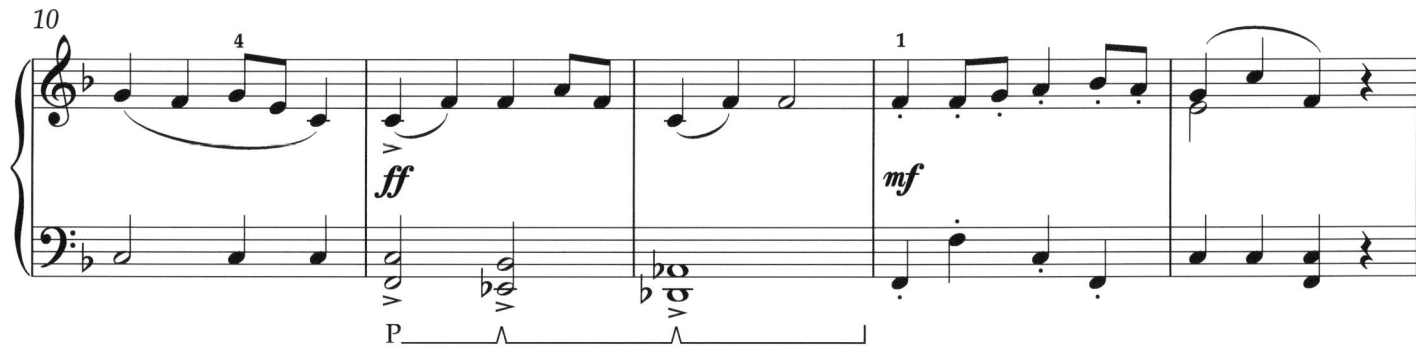
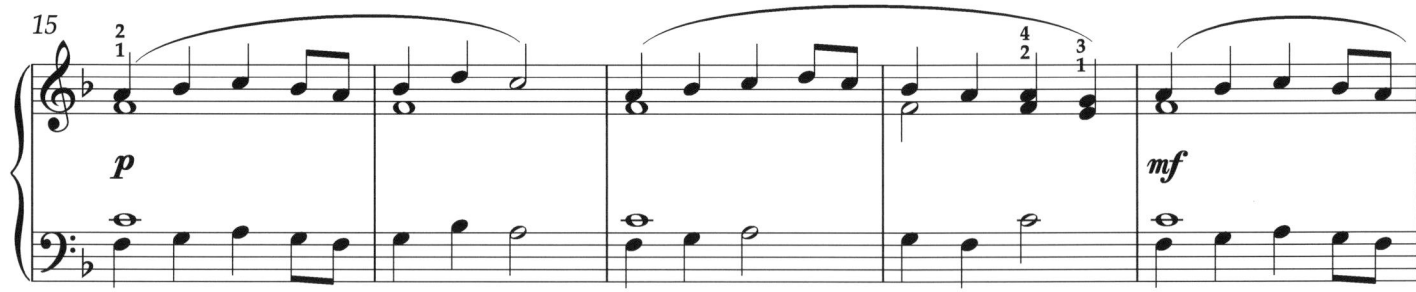
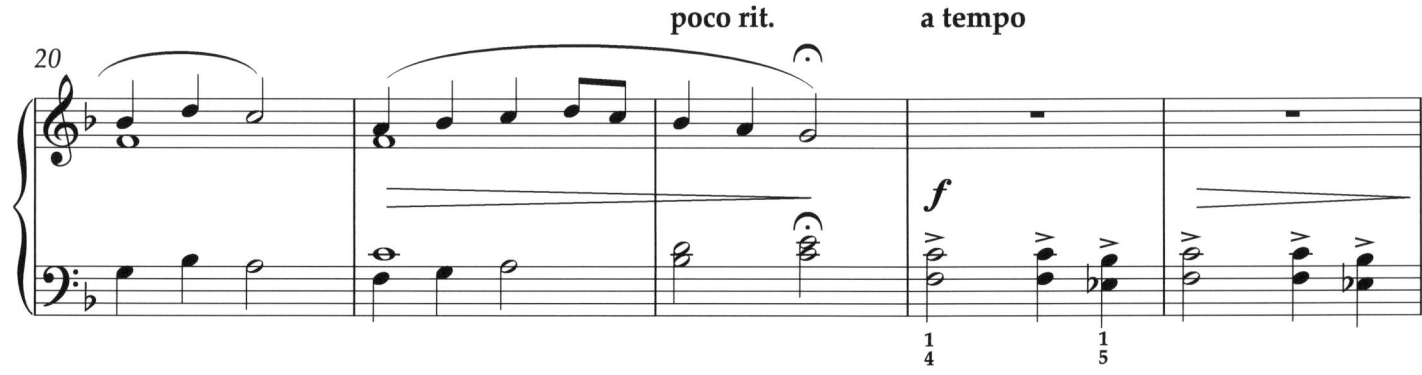

© 2006 by Faber Music Ltd

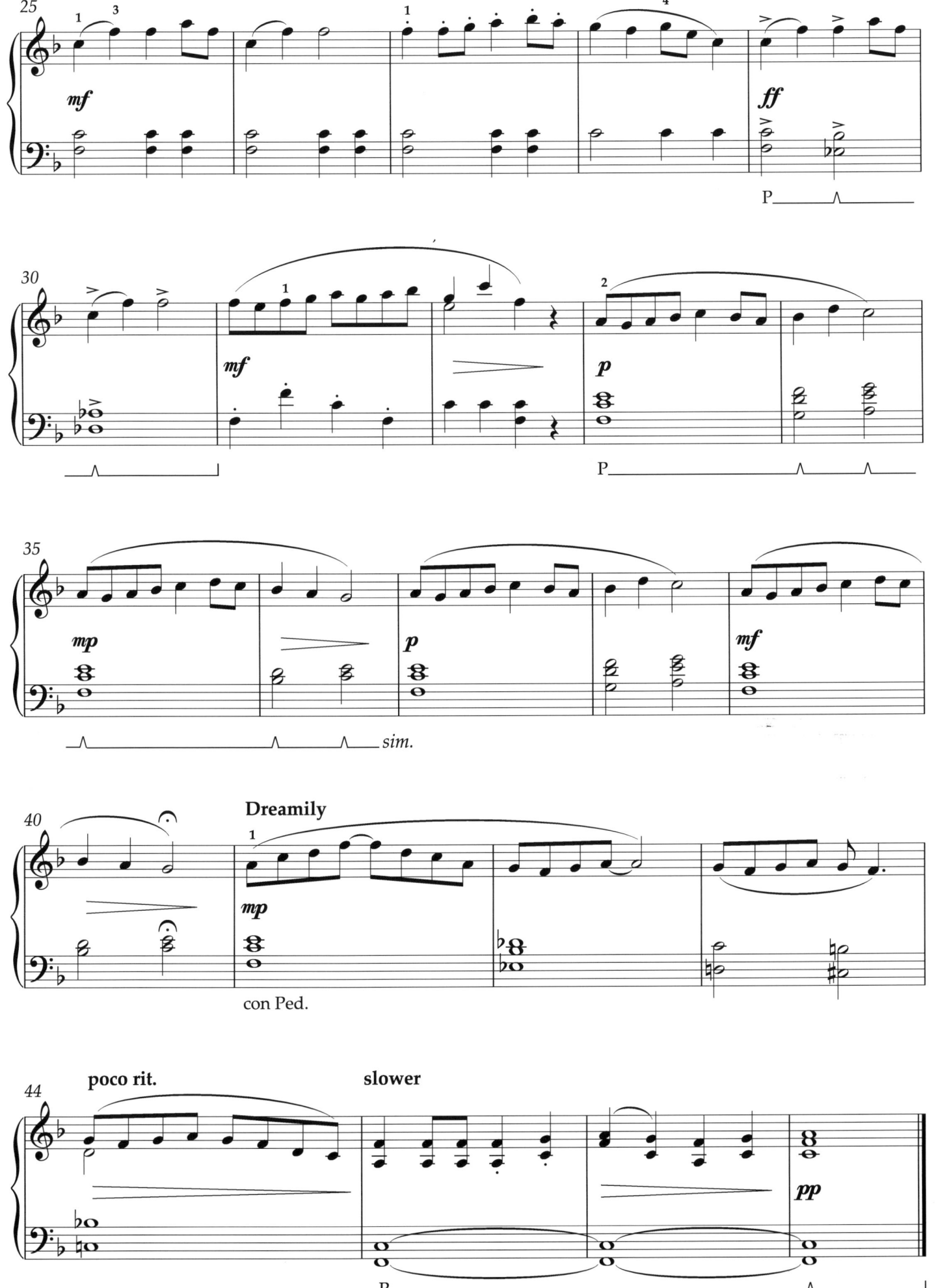

Coventry carol

Renaissance carol

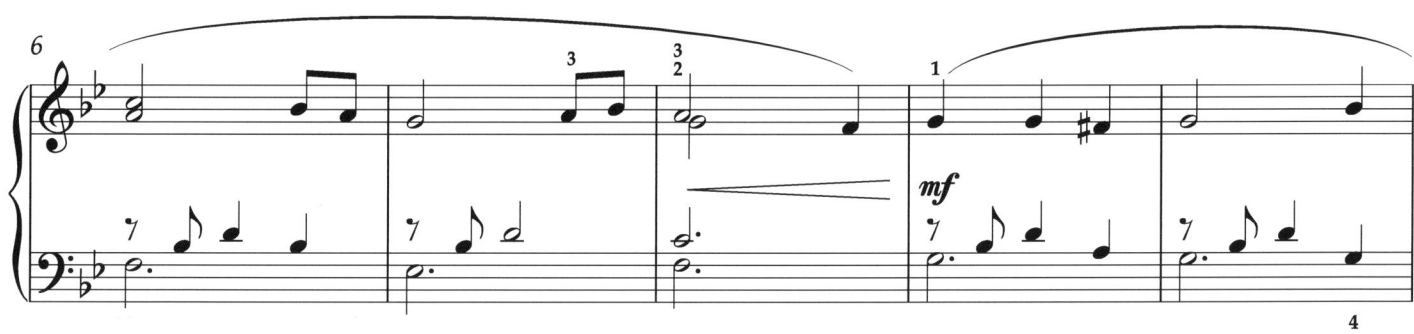
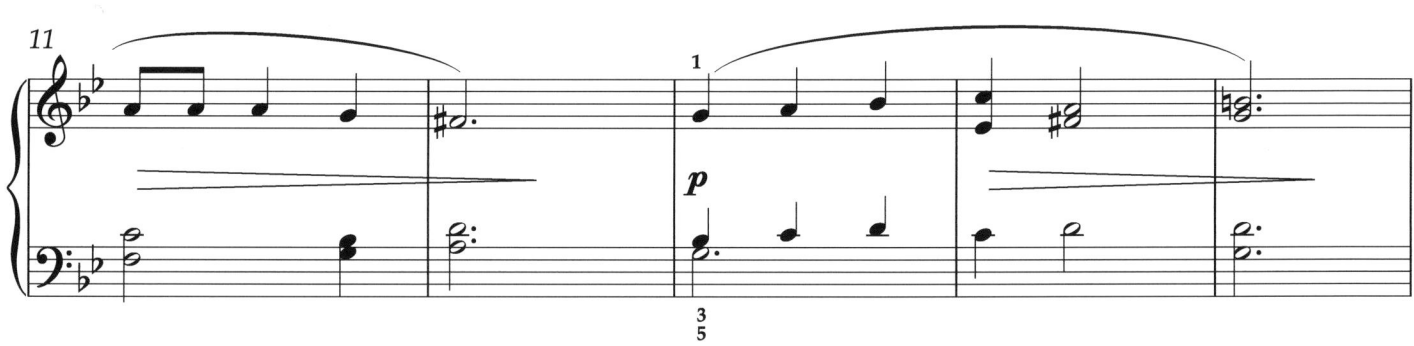

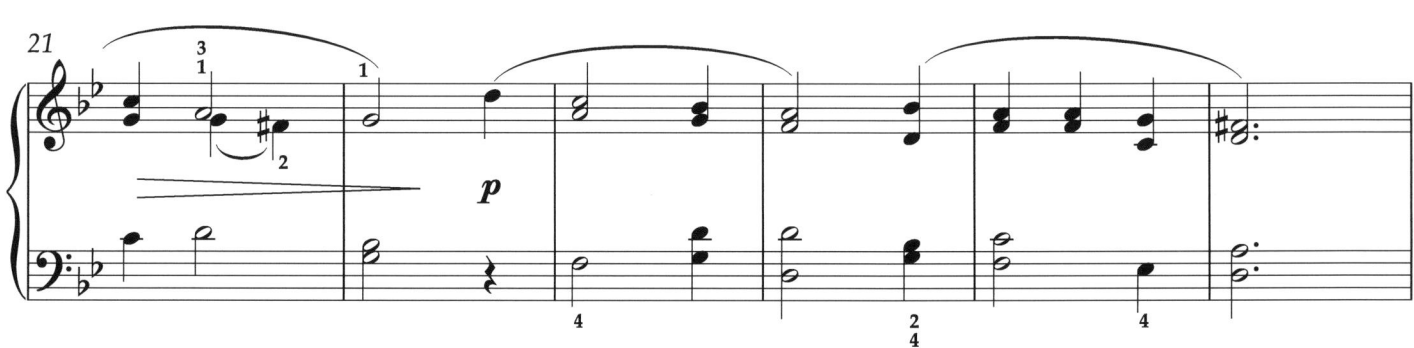

© 2006 by Faber Music Ltd

Ding, dong, merrily on high

Thoinot Arbeau

Joyfully ♩ = 126–132

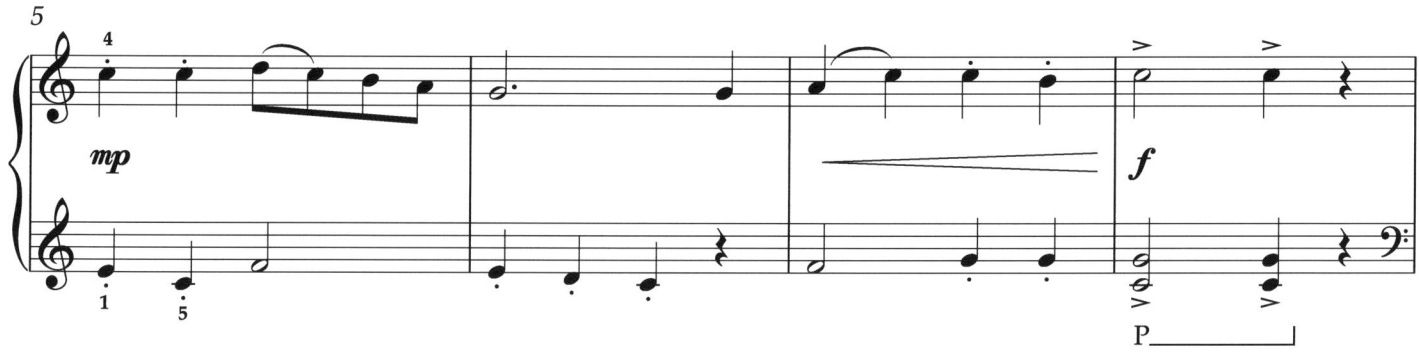

© 2006 by Faber Music Ltd

Walking in the air
Theme from *The Snowman*

Music and lyrics by Howard Blake

At a gently floating speed ♩ = 116

Copyright © 1982 by Highbridge Music Ltd. This arrangement © 2006 by Highbridge Music Ltd
Reproduced by permission of Faber Music Ltd, London. All Rights Reserved

In the bleak midwinter

Words by Christina Rossetti
Music by Gustav Holst

Santa Claus is comin' to town

Words and music by Fred Coots and Haven Gillespie

Quem pastores laudavere

Traditional German carol

Smoothly, with movement ♩ = 120

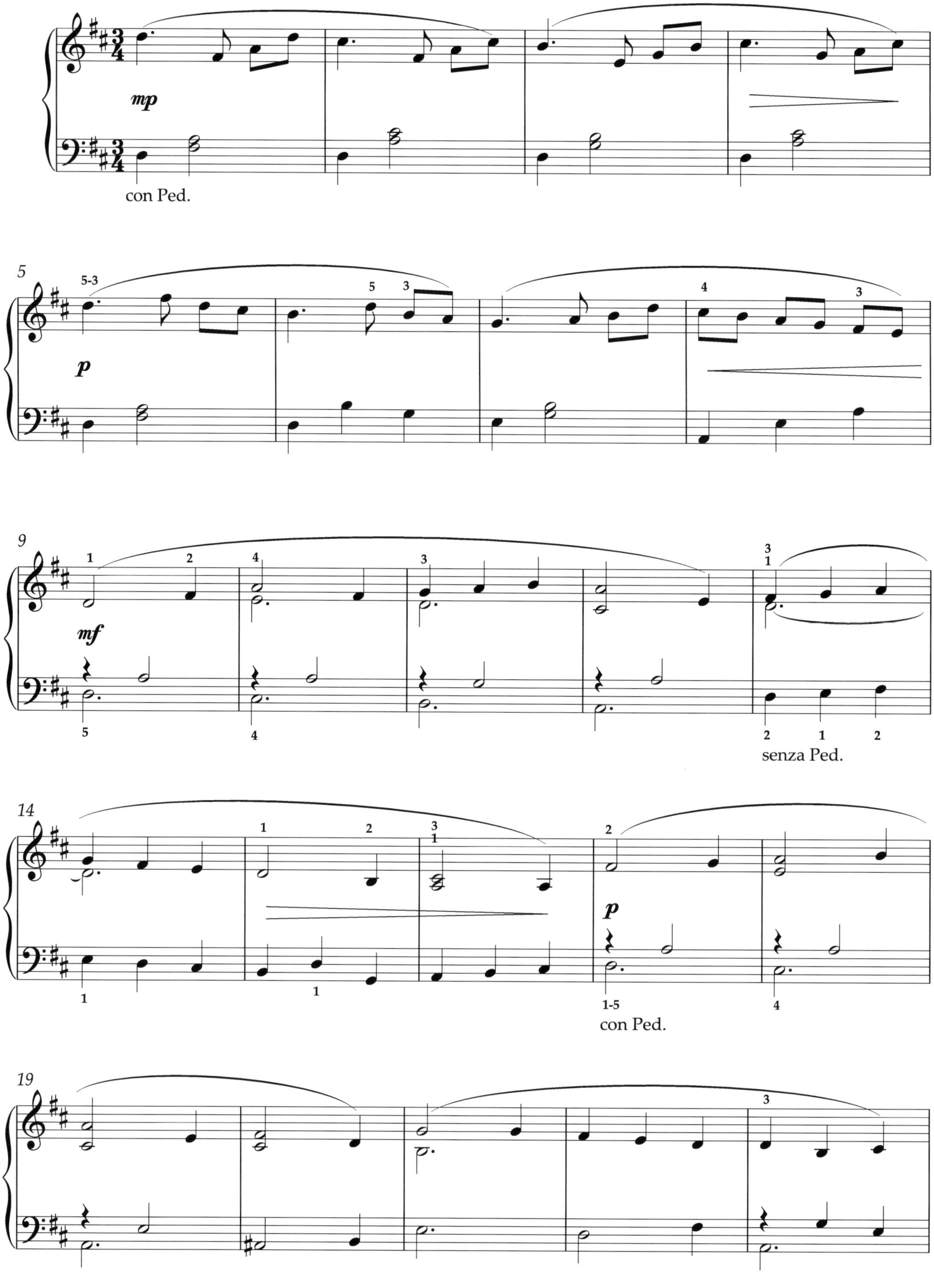

© 2006 by Faber Music Ltd

Christmas song

Words by Robert Wells
Music by Melvin Tormé

© 1946 Burke Van Heusen Inc. Chappell Morris Ltd, London W6 8BS
Reproduced by permission of Faber Music Ltd. All Rights Reserved

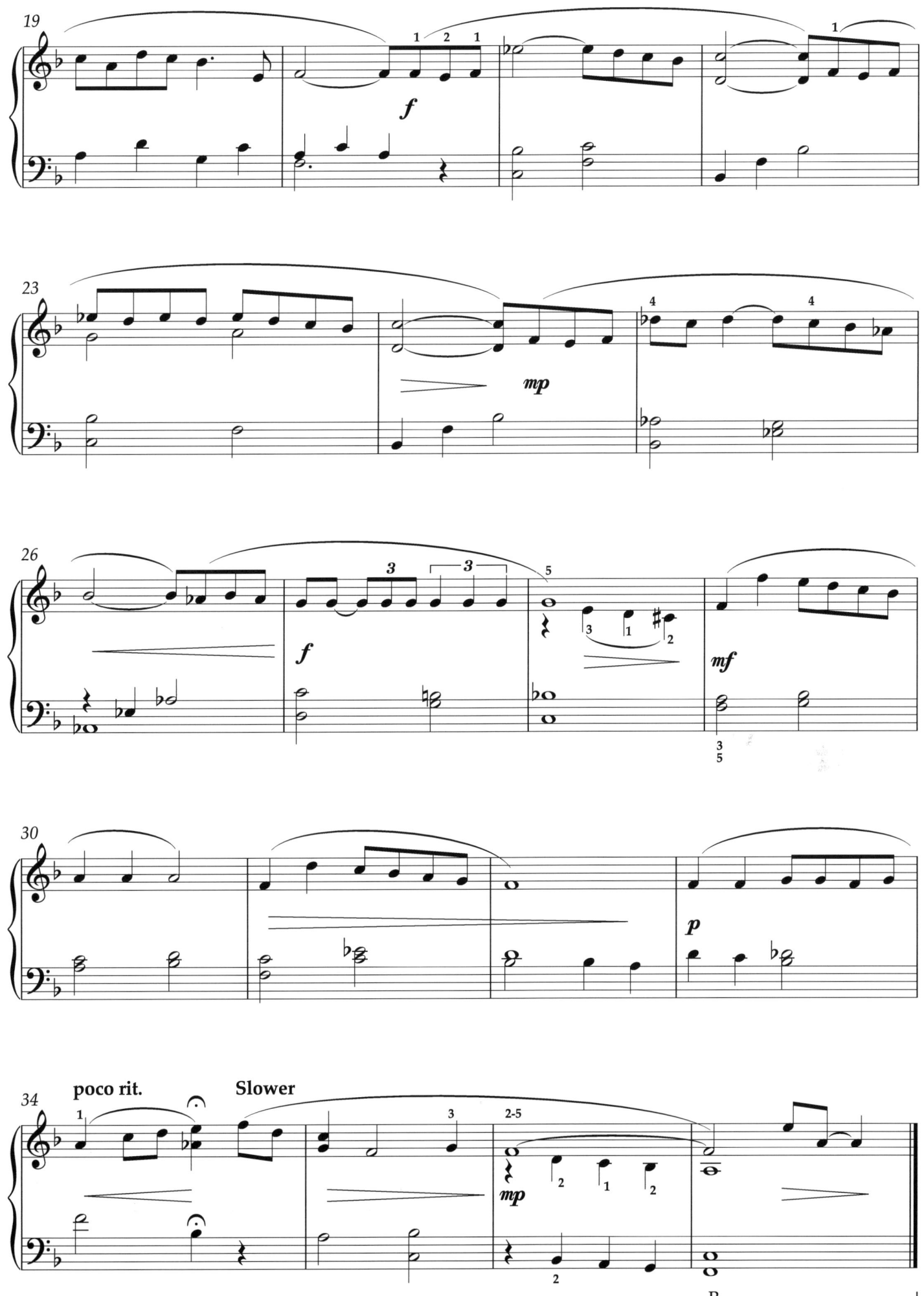

The Virgin Mary had a baby boy

West Indian Spiritual

Calypso style ♩ = 112

Adeste, fideles O come, all ye faithful

Anon

Silent night

Words by Josef Mohr
Music by Franz Xaver Gruber

Winter wonderland: duet

SECONDO

Words by Richard B. Smith
Music by Felix Bernard

© 1934 by Bergman Vocco & Conn Inc USA (50%) Francis Day & Hunter Ltd, London WC2H 0QY (50%) Redwood Music Ltd (Carlin) London NW1 8BD for the Commonwealth of Nations, South Africa and Spain in respect of the 50% interest of Richard B Smith. All Rights Reserved

AFTER HOURS

Alarm clocks, barking dogs, telephones, meetings and rush hour ... the hustle and bustle of life. What better way to relax than to sit down at the piano, chill out and indulge yourself with music from Pam Wedgwood's *After Hours*?

With a variety of pieces in styles to suit any mood—sentimental ballads to cosy dinner jazz, wistful blues to cheerful, upbeat tunes—***After Hours*** provides the perfect antidote to stress. So conjure up the dimly lit atmosphere of a jazz club, and relax with these lush harmonies and laid-back melodies ...

Book 1 *grades 3–5*	ISBN 0-571-52110-X	
Book 2 *grades 4–6*	ISBN 0-571-52111-8	
Book 3 *grades 5–6*	ISBN 0-571-52259-9	
Book 4 *grades 6–8*	ISBN 0-571-53336-1	
Piano Duets *grades 4–6*	ISBN 0-571-52260-2	
Jazz Book 1 *grades 3–5*	ISBN 0-571-52908-9	
Jazz Book 2 *grades 4–6*	ISBN 0-571-52909-7	
Christmas *grades 4–6*	ISBN 0-571-52362-5	
Christmas Jazz *grades 4–6*	ISBN 0-571-53337-X	